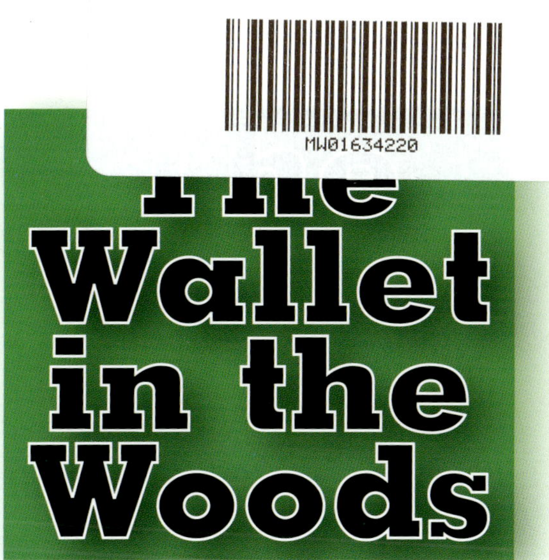

The Wallet in the Woods

by Meredith Costain

illustrated by Chantal Stewart

EDUCATORS PUBLISHING SERVICE
Cambridge and Toronto

Contents

Chapter One

The Field Trip

"Wow!" says Roberto, as our bus rolls through the gates of Big Tree National Park. "Look at the size of those trees!"

The bus pulls into a parking area and slows to a stop. "Okay, class," says our teacher, Ms. Rossi. "I want you off the bus quickly so I can put you into groups."

We're all off the bus, and Ms. Rossi is holding up a folder of project sheets. "Now, class, when you find out what group you're in, I want you to go into the woods and get started." She waves the folder. "I'll be awarding a special prize for the best sheet."

A few of us smile as we imagine winning the prize. We love Ms. Rossi's prizes because they *always* contain chocolate!

Big Tree National Park is famous for its plants. Our class is on a field trip to find out more about them. Each group has to find examples of five different plants. Then we record information about them on our project sheets—things like where they're growing and how big they are. We also have to sketch what they look like.

After we've finished the activity, Mr. Mazur, our physical education teacher, is going to grill hot dogs and hamburgers on the barbecue near the parking area. I can't wait!

"Now be careful and don't wander too far," Ms. Rossi continues. "The park rangers will be keeping an eye on you. Any questions?"

"No, Ms. Rossi," we all say.

Ms. Rossi consults her clipboard.
"Okay. Group One," she announces,
"is Roberto, Lucy, and Adam."

Roberto and I look at each other.
A girl in *our* group?

"And before anyone asks," says
Ms. Rossi, "there is to be *no* changing
of groups. Is that clear?"

Sometimes, I think Ms. Rossi can
read my mind. I look at Roberto and
whisper, "It'll be okay."

He just rolls his eyes and sighs.

Chapter Two

The Search Begins

WHEN WE'RE ALL in our groups, we head off from the parking area. Roberto looks to the left, then to the right. "Which way should we go?" he asks. "Up the hill toward the big rocks? Or down the hill toward the creek?"

"I don't care," says Lucy, shrugging her shoulders.

"The creek," I say, looking at our project sheet. "Some of these plants look like they would grow near water."

"Right," says Roberto. "Let's go."

"I bet you won't find anything on the project sheet," Lucy declares, as we set off down the trail.

Roberto ignores her and stops at some small plants with hooded stalks.

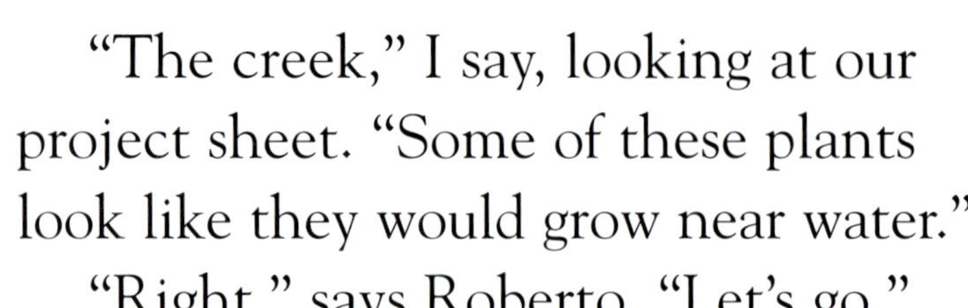

"Look," he says, looking pleased, and pointing to our list of plants. "They look like one of the plants we have to find."

"They are cobra lilies," says Lucy. "My dad showed me one when we went hiking last year. They have a really strange smell."

"Oh," says Roberto, looking impressed. He takes a sniff of the plant, and then wrinkles his nose. Then he looks at me as if to say it might not be so bad having a girl in our group.

"Be careful with that!" A park ranger nearby rushes over to make sure we don't hurt the plant. "They're very rare. I'm Howard, by the way."

"Hi, Howard," I say. "We're being really careful."

I draw a picture of the plant and write notes about its powerful smell. Then we move off down the trail, looking for the next plant. Howard tags along behind us, keeping an eye on us from a distance.

I stop in front of a gigantic tree. I check the project sheet. "Hey," I call to the others. "This must be a dawn redwood."

"Great!" says Roberto.
He and Lucy wait for me
to fill in the sheet,
then we move on.

"Hey, let's check out that valley," says Roberto, wandering off the main trail. "I bet there are some dinosaur ferns down there."

I follow him, but Lucy stays on the trail. "It's too small to be a valley. It's a gully. And I bet there are snakes down there," she calls after us. "I'm staying here."

Roberto watches as I poke around in the undergrowth.

"Hey, look what I've found!" I shout, waving my find in front of his nose.

Chapter Three

An Unexpected Find

IT'S A LEATHER wallet.

"Is there anything in it?"
Roberto asks.

I open the wallet and look inside.
"Not much," I say. "A few dollar bills.
Some old bus tickets."

"Oh," he says, sounding
disappointed. "Anything else?"

Suddenly, a hand reaches out and snatches the wallet from me.

It's Lucy. "What have we got here?" she asks.

"Hey!" I say. "I found it."

I try to get the wallet back from Lucy, but she's holding it too tightly.

"I'm going to find out who it belongs to and return it," Lucy says. "There may even be a reward."

"I don't think so," I say. "Look inside. There's not much in there, and the wallet looks old. Who would bother giving us a reward for returning it? Besides, there's nothing in there to show who it belongs to. There's no driver's license or credit cards."

Lucy opens up the wallet and begins looking through all the hidden pockets. "There *has* to be something."

She pulls out an old black and
white photo. "Wait a minute," she
says. "Look." She passes the photo
to me.

"This must have been taken a long time ago," I say.

"How can you tell?" asks Lucy.

"Well, it looks kind of faded, and look at the old-fashioned clothes they're wearing."

I turn the photo over. Written on the back, in faded ink, are the words *William, Vera, and Gertrude, Mount Eden, 1945.* I read them to Roberto and Lucy. Even the names sound old.

"Maybe the owner of the wallet is one of the people in the photo," says Roberto. "At least we know their names. That's a start."

"Lots of people have those names, so that's not much help. But, if the photo was taken in 1945, the baby would now be a woman in her sixties. Maybe it's her wallet!" Lucy says, looking very pleased with herself. "You found the wallet here, right?"

"Right," I say.

Lucy starts to poke around in the undergrowth. Then she calls us over. "I think I know how to track down the owner. See? I've just found our first clue."

Chapter Four

Searching for Clues

LUCY SHOWS US some marks in the earth. "Someone's been sitting on a stool here. You can see where its legs have pressed down into the ground. And there's another set of marks here, just in front of it."

"What made the second set?" asks Roberto.

"I'm not sure," says Lucy. "But they're not as deep as the first ones we saw. Whatever it was, it's not as heavy."

I start looking around for marks, too. I see something glinting from behind some ferns. It's an old glass jar, with some green stains on it.

"Is this a clue, too?" I ask Lucy.

Lucy takes the jar. "Definitely. I'm not sure what it means, but it has to be a clue."

"Maybe we could take it to one of those crime labs you see on TV," I say, "and test it for fingerprints. If they match the ones on the wallet . . ."

"Well, all that would tell us is that the jar belongs to the same person who owns the wallet," says Lucy.

"Oh well, it was just a thought," I mumble.

Lucy moves off further into the woods. "Now we're getting somewhere," she calls back. She points to a set of footprints that trail up the hill.

"These could belong to anyone," says Roberto. "They're probably from someone in our class."

"I don't think so," says Lucy. "Remember we all had to wear sneakers today? Well, these prints were made by someone wearing cowboy boots."

"Cowboy boots?" says Roberto. "How can you tell?"

"It's the shape of the print," she says. She steps onto the patch of earth so we can see the shape her shoe has left.

"Sneakers have wide soles, with wavy patterns. But cowboy boots have narrow heels and pointy toes—just like this footprint."

"Hang on a minute," says Roberto. "Maybe these prints belong to Ms. Rossi or Mr. Mazur."

Lucy shakes her head. "They're both wearing hiking boots today. Brown, with black laces."

Wow! What a memory! I think.

"So what do we do now?" Roberto asks her.

"Follow the footprints," says Lucy.

"But what about our project sheet?" I say. "Shouldn't we finish it? And what about Howard?" We look behind us at Howard, and give him a cheery wave. He waves back, then tends to some plants by the path.

Lucy rolls her eyes. "Come on. This is more exciting. And maybe we'll find the rest of the plants along the way."

Chapter Five

Solving the Mystery

We follow the footprints until they reach another path that winds around the side of a hill.

"Which way now?" asks Roberto.

Lucy doesn't answer. She is examining the ground around us. She looks to the left for a few moments, then looks at the ground to the right. "This way," she says, pointing to the right.

"How can you be so sure?" I ask.

Lucy points to some marks on the path. "See these? Remember those marks on the ground we saw before? I bet that whatever made those marks was put down here to rest by the person we're looking for."

I bend down to get a closer look. "Hey!" I shout. "There are some green splotches on the ground—the same color that's in that jar I found."

Lucy smiles at me. "Good job, Adam. Okay, let's see where this path leads."

We follow the path for a while.
Tall trees grow thickly on each side.
In the distance I can hear the shouts
of our classmates.

Finally, we walk out of the woods
into a clearing. In front of us is a log
cabin. There's a stool and an easel with
a painting on it. Sitting on the stool
is a woman wearing cowboy boots.

Chapter Six

The Best Prize!

THE WOMAN LOOKS surprised to see us. She drops her brush and green paint splatters everywhere.

"You're an artist!" I say.

"Yes," says the woman. "I'm painting a picture of the woods. Would you like to see it?"

We move a bit closer. Her painting is beautiful. I can see dawn redwood trees, cobra lilies, and dinosaur ferns, just like the ones we saw in the woods.

"Is your name Gertrude?" asks Lucy.

"Yes, it is," says the artist. "How did you know?"

Lucy hands the wallet I found to Gertrude. "We found this in the woods. There's a photo inside of two people holding a baby. I thought the baby might be you."

"My wallet!" exclaims Gertrude. "Thank you so much for returning it. This is the only photo I have left of my mom and dad. But how did you know the baby was me?"

"Simple," Lucy replies. "The photo was taken in 1945, so the baby would be around your age today."

Gertrude smiles. "Well, you're very clever! I'm glad you were in the woods to find my wallet."

Suddenly, I sniff something delicious. It's the smell of grilled hot dogs and hamburgers coming from the other side of the trees. "Well," I say. "We'd better head back now." Roberto and Lucy nod.

Gertrude thanks us again for finding her wallet. And then she does something really wonderful. She gives us her painting of the woods as a reward for finding her wallet. She's signed her name in the corner: *Gertrude Hocking.*

"Wow!" says Roberto. "Ms. Rossi is going to *love* this. Maybe she'll even give us the prize!"

We turn back the way we came, and we bump into Howard, the park ranger. He helps us find our way back to the parking area. We arrive just in time to eat the last of the hamburgers and hot dogs.

We don't win the prize, but something better happens. Ms. Rossi tells us that she's going to hang the painting in the school lobby for everyone to see.

We also decide to write an article for the school newspaper about how we found the wallet and then found its owner. Ms. Rossi thinks that's a great idea.

And you know something else? I'll be happy the next time Ms. Rossi puts Lucy in my group. She's not so bad after all.